REA

S0-BKZ-414

Versus
Exsul

POETRY BY MARIO SUSKO

First Journey (Sarajevo, 1965)
Second Journey or Pathos of the Mind (Zagreb, 1968)
Fantasies (Sarajevo, 1970)
Survival (Sarajevo, 1974)
Confessions (Sarajevo, 1976)
Compositions and Reflections (Sarajevo, 1977)
Land Vision (Zagreb, 1980)
Gravitations, 41 (Sarajevo, 1982)
Selected Poems (Sarajevo, 1984)
Selected Poems (Sarajevo, 1986)
Physika Meta (Rijeka, 1989)
The Book of Exodus (Tuzla, 1991)
A Handbook of Poetry (Rijeka, 1994)
Mothers, Shoes and Other Mortal Songs (Stamford, CT, 1995)
Future Past (Ljubljana, Slo., 1996)
Mothers, Shoes and Other Mortal Songs (Zagreb, 1997)

MARIO SUSKO

VERSUS EXSUL

Post-Word by Ralph Nazareth

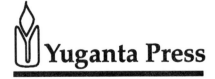

Yuganta Press

Grateful acknowledgment is made to the editors of the
following magazines: *Nassau Review*, *Borderlands: Texas
Poetry Review*, *Kiosk*, *Metamorphoses*, *Parnassus*, *Sulphur
River*, *International Poetry Review*, *The Maverick Press*,
Potato Eyes, *Seneca Review*. Also, thanks to Robert Karmon,
Thomas C. Casey, Bruce Urquhart, Paul Doyle, Barry
Fruchter, John Ostling, Peggy Heinrich, Lynda Sorensen,
and Ann Yarmal for their faithful reading and support.

ISBN 0-938999–12–5
Library of Congress Catalog Card Number
98–060889

First Edition

Yuganta Press
6 Rushmore Circle
Stamford, CT 06905–1029

AN INTRODUCTORY NOTE

Versus Exsul is a programmed book, if one may say so. It consists of poems that the poet extracted from his previous manuscripts, though not in their original sequential order, hoping, almost against hope, that by doing so the poems would somehow presage what the second part, entitled "Exsul," certainly wants to convey. About the "Exsul" portion one of his notes reads, "I must do it this way, not to say only how it happened to me, but to try to see why something that should not have happened did. I do not want to give an account of something but explore whether an account by me would be possible in the first place." Both parts, the first in its sometimes almost feigned simplicity of thought, the second in an often deliberate *tour de force*, manifest the poet's struggle to come to grips with his tragic life and his spiritual drama (a better word would probably be *angst*).

There is a bit of irony in all this. While he was writing in his country of origin, the poet was often accused by his peers of being a "western poet" whose poetry was modeled primarily on American poetic patterns or mode of thinking. Once he, through life's twists and turns, found himself in that milieu, he felt not only literally but also spiritually rejected. He devoted more than thirty years to the culture and literature of a country that, he felt, ultimately rebuffed him. In one of his letters he writes, "I know all too well that I am nobody here as a writer, but I find it utterly devastating that I am also undesirable. This feeling is worse than persecution, since it's like something you know but cannot pin down. I begin to understand why some people here feel they have to do something 'extraordinary,' thus standing a chance to say, 'Yeah, I did it because that was the only way for you to listen to me.' This, unfortunately, has given rise to its absolute opposite, the 'spectacular'—and I say 'absolute' because the 'spectacular' has been turned into the virtual art of shocking, the mere randomness of everything. Once you admit, for instance, that there is such a thing as random killing and treat that as a logical admissibility, you can also find any excuse for it or anything else for that matter. Of course, this does not prove anything; moreover, it can easily be dismissed as the outsider's 'normal' reaction to something he is fundamentally not willing to understand or accept. But, if you fear to retrieve your mail or answer your phone because you feel that someone might have decided that you should stay an alien, both physically and spiritually, you are lost. And those who may say, 'But you haven't done anything wrong, so there's nothing for you to fear,' I can only answer, 'Exactly for that very reason.' Once you are forced to run without knowing why you are being hunted, you never stop to turn round and check whether you have outrun the hunters or if their facial expressions have changed."

Though the poet's letters and notes often seem to be latent exercises in creative intensity, he did live in constant fear that he was going to be exiled to a place where he would vanish without a trace, even more importantly, where his poems would disappear without a trace. He knew what had happened to his library, his manuscripts, lectures, and papers during the war. I have discovered that he sent a copy each of *Versus Exsul* to fifteen people, some of whom he hardly knew. Seven other copies of the partially completed manuscript were, as his notes indicate, sent to other people. This manuscript of *Versus Exsul* was found in Ralph Nazareth's possession, with whom the poet communicated extensively between 1994 and 1998. In a note to him, written on March 30, 1997, the poet writes, "With ravens flopping around me ever so louder, I offer you this incomplete manuscript—there are still five poems to come whose themes I have in my mind. (Am I behaving a bit like Mozart? Ha!) Should something happen to me which is beyond my control, please take care of the manuscript and do not let it go to waste." It is not known whether the present manuscript includes these poems; in another note in his notebook, the poet comments, "*Versus Exsul*—would 60 be enough? Perhaps more than enough. Anyway, maybe even 600 would not be enough, but who would be willing to count (balancing the past and the past)? If something survives a poet, it is a couple of good poems—6 out of 600, 9 out of 900, etc. (I should write less, especially if each poem is slowly doing me in; yet, others may already have taken care of that.)" The present manuscript, incidentally, contains 64 poems.

During my only meeting with Ralph Nazareth several years ago, he dismissed with a smile the notion that the former note ever reached him. By the way, I found him reluctant to talk about the poet, though it was quite obvious that he was very fond of him. He did, however, venture one curious observation, remarking that the poet once said to him, "'You are so much better than I; you manage to control your pain so elegantly, not making yourself vulnerable to every counter punch.'" Ralph Nazareth's "Postword" is a fitting gloss about two individuals whose paths crossed indirectly twenty years earlier, but who then crashed into each other like two birds above the wasteland. One could speculate ad infinitum whether it was the land that caused it or their own flight miscalculation. When I said to Ralph Nazareth that I would like him to finish his piece and that I was willing to include it as it was, he responded in his calm, poetically aristocratic manner, "I want you to know that these recollections, or meditations, may be as much about me as they are about him. I admired his resolve to continue to write and stay deadly serious about his writing, though he must have known that the battle had been lost." And then, I think, he said, smiling almost imperceptibly, something like, "Poor bugger, sometimes he looked to me like some overly updated Don Quixote. Or, which, of course, is even more tragic, because all too real, like a too sober John Berryman. There you see, I'm setting the same old association trap for him."

Before I left, he gave me a poem of his to read, written after he had learned of the poet's arrival out of exile into another kind of exile. Two lines still stick in my mind.

> I must speak to him, match my troubled peace with his grief, what I am with what's become of him.

Finally, we all know that poems should stand on their own. My intent is not to direct a reader or create an atmosphere in advance. It is perhaps a crude attempt to reach outside in order to see what may be inside; or, as Peggy Heinrich voiced it eloquently in her unpublished profile of the poet, "At poetry readings he likes to intersperse his poems with commentary, both of which are laced with sadness and irony. When he tries to lighten up, even his laugh carries an edge of pain. Usually dressed in black from jacket to shoes, his clothes leave me wondering whether this is the costume of a European intellectual or the reflection of an inner landscape."

Jozef Klem

Contents

EXSUL

For all those
Levis, Wats, Józsefs and others
who survived to choose to die

VERSUS

GRAVITATIONS, 41
PHYSIKA META
THE BOOK OF EXODUS
A HANDBOOK OF POETRY

THAT MEANS I WAS

they switched off the light
turned off the water
slaughtered that chagallian rooster of mine
closed the railroad station

That means I was—
to speak to do
to undo

on some feast of being
a history menu—

Now the table's nothing but a betrayal
seasoned with leftovers shadows fingerprints
the dead there merely a tongue-and-eye-pleasure—

And tomorrow a set lunch only
Everything else is the question of supplies
and the waiter's mood.

Truly, like the stomach
the intellect's a habit—even when
the rooster's gone you wake up knowing
someone's always at the door ready
to start crowing

BETWEEN EITHER THIS OR THAT

were it not for this bread and wine
which the old woman puts before me
that thread line on the horizon
would prove to be intolerable,

just like these words,
strung on a piece of paper and dried
by the salty sea air they become
the necessity of the uttered,

equal to hers:
I have no one around, my son,
and I paid for my own funeral,
no one except this one here,
may God have mercy on his soul,

pointing at her dog
that sits motionless beside the table
and harkens with his Kierkegaardian eyes.

THEME VARIATION

There's always a kind of rain—
translators
remaining behind
to justify
the behavior
with a stylistic hand gesture.

There's always a kind of river—
a suicidal run from the source
to the final utterance
where amplitudes of
space wait
bulldozers and sand bags as well.

There's always a kind of sea—
before me sweating
falling at the threshold
of words
gnawing from within like madness
at the bottom of the ominous calm.

INTONING THE INCONGRUOUS

I

so many times we said
"to be"
and here we only
"are"

the eagles strike in us
but wiser we say we are

II

we now have the key
but have lost the doors

III

enough of this musing
when the soldiers' boots
in the night know
where to knock

IV

and I ask you: can pigeons
raised in the attic be
the earthly spies of eagles

INTONING THE ADVANTAGE

maybe the time has come—when
       the shadow on the wall is bigger than I

       the sun on the trigger
       behind my back a silent grin of pursuers.

I'll stand like this till the nightfall
all ears immobile like a lizard's head
stuck out cautiously between two stones—

I know that come a flash
he'll be faster.

Because they'll want me to turn round—
thus everything will be justified:
there was a motion
the challenge of recognition
a reflex reaction—

Because without thinking someone
has already signed on the dotted line.

That means having an advantage
       my dear lizard
everything by the rule and
according to God's law

(after all you know that better than I)

THE SPICES & THE PURPOSE

I shall not go to my own funeral
with my face tightened back
already a lighthouse to bugs
to leaf pictures in my eyes
to find winter feed in my ears
negotiate about a soul in my nostrils

I still haven't digested a philosophy of agreement
I still wage war on white mountains
I still let the wolves know where the snares are
though I'm increasingly afraid of the sheep in the valley

of famous speakers with false teeth
indifferent conductors with starched collars
physicians with future finality:
everything-is-going-to-be-fine-do-not-worry.

It doesn't matter what they'll throw on me:
dirt embers or absolutely Nothing

God is I know the greatest coward
who masked that well with a man's fate.
Yet, there's something missing here—
maybe a pinch of salt and pepper?

SOBERING UP

Too long have I defied the oblivion of wisdom
too long in the turn of time searched for the wisdom of
        oblivion

This hand that reaches no further than a dog's chain
is somewhere between: the willingness and clenched teeth

I have changed not a single bird not a single wall
they still remain the mass in the space of their own volume

and maybe that's a given perception—you are matter
that stays a matter which in the end somebody something
opens with a perfect proportion of splitting
along the inner seam—thus redeeming
parts of reason from the insanity of memory.

Then this madness is a final sobering up
the final dying of words before the needle law
the utter quietness of nerve the ultimate joy of silence.

RIVER MELANCHOLY

I cannot sit on the bank any more
and cheat the river with stories of eternity

if in this space I'm nothing but
a bridge builder trading across the water
with one eye at the water level
the other at the hide map.

The river madness is a desert abundance of nothingness
since the latter never an appropriate boundary
though a defiance always forcing the conquerors
to think of themselves of the mortality of their acts.

I know now
there was too much symbolism in your courses
too many smug fishermen
with tales of dimensions

and the cause of all that is always something else
under the surface unacceptable to its own circumference.

Like creation
you exist only as a surplus of endurance.

(PHYSIKA META, 1)

the present time of necessity:
a square table, a plastic flower in a vase—
the bee's patient circling around illusion:

is life
nothing but an art of deception (?)—

seventy guests at breakfast,
eating bread with butter and honey—

the future time of chance:
a frantic hermit or forerunner that finally
has to taste its own remade self:

is art
nothing but a deception of life (?)—

a hand moves up and closes the window,
and then, after the last bite, a zigzagging
madness on the glass of eternal appearance—

(PHYSIKA META, 2)

it seems to me—or so the others want—
a lemon drop squeezed into the eye on the plate,
and the fish winks at me—
an apple in the rosy snout,
and the pig smiles at me—

there's something in those heads
that come to a table,
as if they refuse to acknowledge death—

meanwhile I speak all my life
for thus I think I breathe,
though I know: words are ever faster,
the breath ever slower—

and all my life I stare at dots
for thus I believe that something's moving,
though I know: the waves charging at me
only belie the stillstand of high seas—

(PHYSIKA META, 3)

then—you know:
it was enough to step out of your dream,
cross the railroad tracks and descend to the hut,
empty except for a bed, with an army blanket
on the window—and there, before the door,
tempting fate: crow at the top of your lungs—

well—can you:
fork every muscle of your childhood,
long gone—since morning, yesterday, the hand
measuring the last word, since tomorrow: and speak,
name—the father sleeping under the stone, leave

the watch in the oven—and know:
this much breath to inhale before silence,
this much to exhale before final answers,

to get to the bone, and keep the balance—

knowing,
all adjectives have already flown down south,

(PHYSIKA META, 4)

this meal is going on a bit too long
this meat is still oozing blood—

my father's nothing but a dehydrated mass
in a chalky frame,
the table the plate the fork in the heart—

this tearing of memory
with my teeth knows no end—

the bones cannot rearrange one's dreams,
this hide crucified on the wall
is but a bait to measure the soul—

for, the guest sitting across from me
will not materialize in a photograph

(PHYSIKA META, 5)

now that my blood slowly rots in my feet
it's too late to look for a flame in open fields,
to travel to new words with beads, fruit, mirrors—

now that a sentence length means the amount of lungs'
          breath,
what truth does this toothless mouth have the right to,
while the tongue insanely turns around daily mortality—

now that the last password rays vibrate in tree crowns,
what insanity can these eyes hope for
that never stood before a sight of their own—

you sit at the table and you know: this silence
will not confuse oblivion—one should have got up perhaps
and left, taken an ashtray—and thus bribed the memory.

(PHYSIKA META, 6)

Nothing can save me any more
From this Weight—I'm ever so close to the Earth—

The embrace of final inertia
Of Flight and Return—the maddening reason—

Let it then be so—if the sky
Betrays me, the Sea does not—

Rolling on the surface the Mass of its own Death—
While measuring through itself the patience of the Eternal—

I have nothing more to say—superfluous at this table—
Like a good child I've cleaned my plate

And held my tongue—
The only thing left to do is to Forget to Breathe—

(PHYSIKA META, 7)

when he stepped off the photograph
he couldn't remain our child any longer—
he could not sit at this table, eat this heart.

when he threw the sun into the oven,
trying to flee his own shadow—
we sentenced him to live his burnt dreams.

when he affixed an eagle's beak to a swallow
and smeared with clay our calendar days—
we left him in the field with butterfly wings.

when he began to hang nightingales' tongues
on trees, we gouged out his eyes
and waited for him to start finally to sing.

(PHYSIKA META, 8)

history is bones, stories are meat—
what remains is the choice through oblivion
—like eternity;
all journeys are in the warehouse, dismantled
into syllables—
in the living room, on the couch, the nouns
of fate sleep snugly—

truth(is/of)truth(of/is)truth(is):
the curse of a place—verbs—of existence
of motion—behind the doors,
for those who are credulous enough—because
of hope—the inflection of consciousness—

but meager is the age in auxiliary verbs,
like a muscle that contorts around the spear's tip

—in me,
and for me, to keep silent while speaking—

(THE BOOK OF EXODUS, 1)

let us say
if life is a story
of pulling a rabbit out of a hat
and a story life
of a rabbit pulled out of a hat

what's more important for the maker:
a hat a rabbit or maybe the audience—

for a real hat the rabbit is a conjuring
for a real rabbit the hat is an illusion

but then:
what would life be were there no hope
of the audience that a rabbit might really be there
and what would a story be were there no belief
of the maker that the rabbit is and isn't there—

so much of:
life and story
the maker and the audience
the truth and the magic
the hide and the drum
death and immortality
and so on and so on and

(THE BOOK OF EXODUS, 2)

father of mine
who art waiting on the horizon
with your left eye shut
we've said
we make peace in this story

should I now again
look for a stick
and tell my rabbit
let's take it one more time
from the top
with a bit more fortitude

all I remember I remember
perhaps as the life's oblivion
in words that resist the moment
of the doors opening

when everything bursting out
falls into a possessive

maybe I should have learned
of the terms of understanding

the point we meet at
always marks a perfect symmetry
of a trigger and breathing: the peace
where the light explodes

(THE BOOK OF EXODUS, 3)

in what possible curve of oblivion
does this hand see me while I beat with
a snake-like stick upon the waters

my dying will again be nothing
but comedy for there is no maker
in this story to guarantee the truth

of magic there is no innkeeper either
to draw a wayward line
under the memory or a character

to show the river a purpose for moving
in the nature of a text: there then
to thrust forth the deafness of my bloodstream

—for words like these one should find
a new story or some other river

(THE BOOK OF EXODUS, 4)

(as to the [strategic] questions)—

have I invented a river
to run away from the father
has the father created me
to set his spirit free

have I sacrificed my rabbit
all too quickly to justify the purpose
of moving and he knew from the beginning
that the story had no real ending

or is reality the hand repeating
history while damming the water
and putting a period where a breath
can sustain words no longer

have I then exchanged my self for the eye's
supreme fiction that wants to see the nature's
curve when the hand writes out
the soul's last measure

          —(and answers)—
when the left imagines what the right is doing
          —(the chorus sings)—
(hahahaha):(ahahahah)

(THE BOOK OF EXODUS, 5)

                    (enter a new character;
                    a monologue follows:)

you bring me in now, at this moment,
because the action loses in tempo
and in the funhouse rabbits stare perplexed
at the multiplication of their images

while you stand in the middle of a river
holding a ball and grinning at the sky,
you need me as a witness,
a counterbalance to figures on the bank
with fragrant erasers in their hands,

and perhaps I myself am a rabbit:
a hero and a victim,

for I know, your only hope was
that the word order proved the mind order,
that the real were the assumed which made you
be in the imagined point of confluence—

but, laughter is never a free energy
for the mass, nor, when the boundaries of
oblivion are dreamed out, is it possible
to flee from the geography of a text—

(THE BOOK OF EXODUS, 6)

for a rabbit the purpose of existence is
to multiply its own image
thus through the sheer volume of survival
it seeks to baffle its Maker

—but the end is so prosaic
the latter flashes light in its eyes
the rabbit stops like frozen
and drops dead (that too when you
are not a deer or a cow
and do not have a road sign of your own)

—yet the flash could be the final knowledge
of the unbalanced measure of power—a point
which a word cannot flow over and
wander off beyond the flat atlas—

who is then to forgive whom
—the one who draws fate lines or
the one who wants to trick the Maker
with stories of infinitude—

(you ask now what was all that for,
about God and a rabbit—
I do not know, it looked like a good parable
—and yet, remember how you naively
stretched your palm and how they taught you
to dream and forgive—)

(THE BOOK OF EXODUS, 7)

a hand draws a line
      the line feels the hand
the hand doesn't ponder the line
      the line changes the hand

the hand pulls a trigger
      the energy doesn't know the hand
the motion assumes a target
      the eye divides a mass

the hand erases the line
      the line remembers the hand
the hand's a gauge imaging infinitude
      the line sees the hand's finitude

the hand releases the trigger
      the eye forgets the mode
the nerve still envisions the motion
      but materializes in the other mass' body

the easiest thing then is to remember
      what you do not recall

(THE BOOK OF EXODUS, 8)

1.   still so many stories left and so little life
1a.   so many interpretations a story has and just one life

2.   life needs a story with a beginning a middle and an end
2a.   a story presupposes a life that hangs on its end

3.   life traces the motion of the mass
3a.   a story wants to be the cause of the mass' energy

4.   life can always run into a story to save its head
4a.   a story cannot flee into life to change its head

5.   a story always borrows from life and changes nothing
5a.   life always steals from a story and denies the illusion

6.   is the rabbit happier in the hat
6a.   is the hat denying the rabbit's maker

7.   and so on
7a.   and on so

(A HANDBOOK, 1)

to begin I'd have to start—
not with a word that binds
(for if I say: there'll be no rabbits
that means: there'll be no hunters either
and the whole sequence reacts accordingly)
with a force of horizontal progression—

to begin I'd have to fall—
in the question of the hand and the finger
of direction and the curve of remembrance
(and now I'd need again
two big parallel
counterposed life-giving words)
of some vertical decree—

(for all this I'd need a father ready
to stand with him at some beach and stare
at the universe that runs past me unmoving)

(this then a true beginning would be
and I could step out of a poem unscaled)

(A HANDBOOK, 2)

perhaps this is a good beginning (assuming
the consciousness' circumference is the eye's range): true
          words
are those that teach you to comprehend the past / new line /

of future—though this too may seem deluding
for all to bes and not to bes we grew up with—
too late (if breathing is an antidote for words) for all

freed too early: when you fail to muse that
which muses you, strayed into an erroneous fate, the present
tells of only as much reality as you can digest.

(A HANDBOOK, 3)

of all you wanted to imagine as the beginning
—of a poem or a life it doesn't really matter—
you see only the encrusted words
someone plucks the vowels out with tweezers

—all those parts that demand a purpose
though never guaranteeing it its permanence

—nouns that in a dream come out of your mouth
like earthworms and in the morning you find
your mouth smells of milk and garlic

—can you do anything with a consonant memory
when you open your mouth and step out of a singular—

the beginning of life is to exchange yourself
with some other self
the beginning of a poem is to exchange yourself
with your own self

—the measure of consciousness is speech
even when they cut off your tongue and you start
to talk about yourself with your eyes only
the consciousness of speech a test measure
when through repetition you try to be
a plural and thus the majority of a beginning—

can a stative verb then still hope
to reveal the illusion of a taste muscle

the *waswillbeistobewas*   (being?)

(A HANDBOOK, 4)

if like germs these words could
survive under the snow and then
in spring sprout awakened anew
innocent and defiant like a woman

if I could come like a shower
earth and soak your chapped lips
wash off the walls all greasy eternities
and laugh at the cases of their faith

then every poem could easily
fend for itself and my hand be free
to hold moisture in a tuft of breath

but these words are increasingly like milk
to a dead son in swollen breasts
I cover with a cabbage leaf as solace

(A HANDBOOK, 5)

is it possible to forgive those
that do not know how to forgive

those that take a word to be
the dead's revenge   (against

the living? as the overplowed dirt
avenges itself with weeds)

those that grew up watching
dung vaporize in the morning
field as breath of the resurrected

those that silently observe
the ashes white as pulverized bones

—can here the words of becoming
equal there those of dying

here the memory reap nouns
of that which there was sowed as verbs

or the answer is not to be found
until I like a smiling sun in the shooting
gallery drop happy below the horizon

(A HANDBOOK, 6)

all this is pretty naive my dear
—the beginning which is a harkening
of a conception which (and a possible
word here would surely have to be the
light) according to a measure of hearing

—but what is predictable for somebody
who sees the dead hour of the day

if you cannot go further than life
that starts exploding in the membrane

never able to reconcile behind the
doors your own self with that which winks
at the sun in the reflection of a heavenly womb

—which again—when you switch things round—is
but a dot pulsating in a dead pond—

apart from it everything's a blank wall
in which you search in vain for a hollow
of the first sight knowing that our eyes
are opened only by witches ghosts or blindmen

(A HANDBOOK, 7)

Twilight. When the eye widens. When the soul shrinks.
Looking for a stronghold. In the space of an unseen leap.

"What do you think, how far till we're there?" you ask.
"Two hundred meters," I answer readily.

As if I had already been there. Spent the night.
The insect knowing exactly the distance to its victim.

Had I been? Having purposefully forgotten everything.
After the prey had been captured and desecrated.

Shall I recognize? Be recognized?
The hand in the pocket reaching tremblingly through the air.

The soul is already there at the window, inviting,
Like a whore in those black-and-white movies.

I wait in the dark. When the body stumbling
Can hope that crashing into somebody is just an embrace.

(A HANDBOOK, 8)

this land that I devour devours me, unaware
we're both weighed down with the same load.

at midnight our plates are piles of shiny bones,
shanks necks ribs skulls wings.

and when realizing that so heavy
we can't fly off anywhere, we switch to coloring.

we gulp down the yellows, reds, browns,
soft, hard, gluey, until we go blind.

then, finally, the colors are all one shade, and
we even have the same number of bones on the plates.

we exchange them taken by the creation.
the land makes me, I, the land, till the morning.

Muster me westward fitter to my end—

EXSUL

BUT THE TRUTH

Everyone says that I'm
a valuable witness.
To what? Truth, you say?

Truth is no longer naked.
It wears designer clothes
created on some Sunrise Avenue
and stitched together in some
Jamarta, San Singo, Getucipalga.

Truth is no longer plain.
It's like sophisticated fake jewelry
on a fabulously rich woman.
You either know it's fake but say
nothing aware that she can afford
the real thing, or you don't want
to know because no matter what you say
she makes others believe it's real.

Truth is no longer justice
for the latter does not imply
an apt symmetry of fortune.
Truth is reality on the ground.

And there on the ground a gander
refuses to fly off south because of
two magnificent plastic geese
they planted in to make the pond pretty.

Do you detect some bitterness
in all this? You do? You are right.
Do you feel there may be poetic justice
in what I say? Not really? Right again.

A POEM WITH A REFRAIN
                              (OR
A MEMORY TRIP ON I95
GOING HOME FROM A POETRY READING
WITH 70 BOOKS IN A BOX
FLANKED BY THE SPARE AND THE JACK)

—two wicker chairs on the street
equidistant from the curbs
a lean skinned tree trunk across
and a cardboard nailed in the middle
with scribbled dripping black letters:
checkpoint Republic of sbh—

> *this is the age of*
> *instant history*
> *its makers are now*
> *part time prophets*

—in the uncut grass behind
the house with flies above
like dots against blue canvas
a young corpse an AK-47 wedged
between levi's legs his adidas
feet pointing outward and
a sweatshirt flashing the words:
we are the champions—

> *this is the age of*
> *instant history*
> *its makers the bones*
> *of future hostages*

—there was a poet once quoted
some major saying: we had to destroy
the village in order to save it
—today another major plays
the same practical oblivion
proclaiming he's permitted to talk
with the war crimes general
because he doesn't speak with him
directly but through an interpreter—

> this is the age of
> instant history
> its makers once again
> lethean dustmen

OF SPEAKERS AND TEACHERS (WITH A P. S.)

In that land
people would buy
a cemetery plot
well in advance
and then die
in some cabbage patch
some corn field
thinking that way
they widened the boundaries
of the living.

> The present was always
> in the future which
> always was in the past
>
> Paradise is just round the corner
> a speaker would blare
> across the muddy coal-field village
> one only has to recognize it.

> > Perhaps it jumps us
> > unprepared a teacher would comment
> > and then over the summer carry
> > stones on some island
> > from the west to the east and back again

P. S.   The teacher did not have a plot
and no one knew where he had vanished
having one day smashed with a stone
the speaker in the village square—
Some claimed he had gone

to the mountain to live with eagles and snakes
others contended that that was nothing but
his way of defying a historical progress.

PUTTING IT RIGHT

(a short list of war idioms,
not a poem—certainly not
a lyric poem)

1.
They wouldn't hurt a flea
        so they burned the whole village.
2.
Being sitting ducks
we all ended up in   a duck soup.
3.
We had everything   once   from
soup to nuts.   (And some bolts.
4.
Then we ate like a bird
        and each shell killed two of us.
5.
There's a grenade in my soup.
        Well,   eat   and   run.

6.
We waited for them to drop   the other shoe.
                        It came cruising.
7.
It pays to get your foot in the door.
(Even more to get your tank.
8.
Beating the gun with sticks and stones is fun If
you know where you can stick you neck   out.

9.
They threw everything at us   including
the kitchen sink.   And some Drano.
10.
If you paid an arm and a leg for your life
you might go to America for prostheses. (See Disneyland)

11.
We took them in.
          They   took   us   out.
12.
They wanted to blow us to smith/ere/ens
          so their guns left no stone unturned.
13.
Then they pulled the plug on us.
(Big deal!   The hospital was without power anyway.
14.
We poured oil   on troubled water.
          Then   they struck a match.
15.
Their obsession was to go down in history.
Mine,   to go up   in historicity.

OF SIGHT AND SANITY

In this other world
the snowy suburban landscape
at seven p.m. almost conjures
some invisible sniper to shoot
me and end the slow motion memory

I do not watch TV news
afraid that I might recognize
myself riddled with bullets
over two greenish potatoes
and a box of damp matches
though I know that here
one dies only for cash value

I do not cross bridges
afraid that I'd have to reinvent
myself at the other end
while watching my mother offer
her wedding ring to guards
to let her cross over

I try to make others believe
that I am still sane, and I am,
as long as I keep my eyes open

OF WRITING POETRY
IN A COUNTRY WHERE
CARS TALK & FROGS DRINK BEER

A man with bifocals came up to me
and said, "I have a problem with
your suffering. A shell is a shell,
and if you survived it to relive it
in poetry, why all the indirectness—
fluorescent light blinding you with
its dilatation, is that to intimate
a ferris wheel's neon explosion you
once stared at, a boy transfixed?
Make me see it the way I too would see
it. Only then will I be able to take it."

       Let us say, you see a blind man in
the street; his hand tilted, a plastic cup
poised (crookedly?) in his hand, he stands
in front of a store (jewelry store?), a dog
next to him stares at a grey hydrant. (Grey?
For whom, you'd say, if one can be there
in the first place?)
               I see the dog with
a rope around its neck, the other end wound
round the blind man's wrist;
       my dog looks at the hydrant (which I
put there), at the eyes behind dark glasses
(yes, there are dark glasses), each time
the cup shakes the coins, wanting still
to move towards the object of its color-
less desire, and blaming me for the rope's
shortness.

In my poem, the dog, the blind
man, their eyes (the eyes that do or do not
see) are a blindness remembering my sight.
A sight becoming aware of my blindness.

Poetry is just that: the inverted
mind
perceived, plus/minus a descriptive
blind
man/feeling.

"You see," the man said, "poetry must be
a story experienced, just like life itself.
What you need are good glasses; and, by
the way, do not try to turn what I said
into some kind of poem," leaving me before
the everything-must-go jewelry store, with
a piece of rope round my left/right hand,
the imaginary/real dog at my side, and,
yes, his bifocals in my plastic cup.

POINT OF CONTACT

What was I doing at the center
of that gravitational lunacy

Words seemed to be different
though the music was the same
Or was it the other way round
And after all did it matter

—now on this sandy promontory
I am but the maker's tangent
while the sea nibbles at my feet
and I pretend to have outrun
the dead sound's circumference—

I know the waves too will betray me
touching the arc of another drum beat
as floodlights on the slope get ready
to laugh at the candle in my hand and
the little red dot like crosswires is
already fixed at the back of my head

THE $_{\text{/WAR/}}$ ^{AS}

to be
as
the as of being

see the blood and the mud
as
a strawberry chocolate cake

to see the dead before the wall
as
the living behind the wall

break a slice of bread in half
as
a magician that makes it stay one

circle round your body
as
a tenseless copula

to be in a nut shell
as
the not shall be

SEIN UND DASEIN

SHALL MY LEG BE
    this leg

once removed from
    BEING

a leg
THAT LEG BE
again

ONCE
twice removed from
THE BEING

away from me
be anew
an image

just a leg
of some the
me

immaterial
here

there

the nerve that dies
in memory

like a thought

the wood knocked on
meeting echo

in hollowed

screaming

silence

DEATH: TWO POEMS

One.

  I've danced with Death,
  My feet wirebrushes on the mahogany floor,
  My eyes wide open, colorless.

  And I was in awe. Even now
  I still feel the splendor of the moment when I
  Realized she'd been sent by Him.

Two.

  I've slept with Death,
  Let my mouth swallow her semen
  Breath that like a blast left my blood airless.

  And I saw my body scatter,
  A bunch of deflating red balloons,
  Their whizzing sound coming to or going out of my mind.

Three
Vaporized light. in memory.
Only, the air. verbless. Flash Faces. Photographs
of dimensions. Nameless.

nouns. Tagged skulls. Future
history decorations. colors of the mind. Restitched
flags. Witnesses. short-sighted punctuation marks.

And still nothing. No
Revelations. that they danced with themselves.
that they slept with their own eidolons.

FOUR BEATS

to harvest a heart
in the field of ebbing ears

to have a young girl carry it
in her apron like warm spongy bread

rays of light behind a spun cloud
to sift through the eye of a needle

while bodies lie clamped by steel caterpillars
with tufts of hair quivering in the wind

*

In her room the girl touches with her forefinger
The open heart on a faded picture.

The soldiers sit in a bar in the village square
Drinking red wine and trading plundered souvenirs.

Tomorrow an olive plane will bring blue men
To mark boundary ridges and disinfect the valley.

*

Can I, far away, standing at the end of this jetty
Start over with a heart that remembers nothing?

A red balloon draws illegible messages
In the sky. I hear a girl cry on the beach.

I'll get it, I yell. And mother whispers behind me:
You're not to go in till they clear the mine field.

*

fretful crows hop around picking dried clots
mindless of crossarmed strawmen rising in the air

the girl turns the wrong way in her sleep
stepping into the orange flare that spreads her legs

and hurls her disremembered heart
after little black tatters

SONG OF SUNNY

every night I go out
hoping my blood will slow

down to the point of throbless
stillness that washes away

memory and a flickering
speck on the retina's horizon

nothing to be retrieved by
breathing nothing in the mirror

in that glassy dead calm words
I know would have to forget me

and I wouldn't need to begin
each howling morning standing

at the edge of land till my mind
goes raucous and the optic nerve

makes out that even a spectral
dog couldn't swim across the ocean

GUNS AND THINGS WE DO, AGAIN

My own words seem strange to me now.
I have to learn to smile again.
But first I have to learn to say them.
And here the odd word is *again*.
They say they'll fix my teeth.
I still feel the cold smooth barrel.
In my mouth it smells like onion.
Or is it the hand protruding out of darkness.
I imagine I am cracking young walnuts.
And I remember my first water gun.
My aunt sent it to me, transparently blue.
You could see through, its veins and joints.
I sprayed all the girls in my street.
It was like orgasm, the holding off, the release.
The same electricity I feel now in my testicles.
Again is, then, not such a peculiar word.
Nor is *encore*, *bis*, anew, *da capo*.
A woman appears, blonde like a fairy,
Lifts her skirt and flashes her dark forest.
I remember my classmate at the cemetery
Showing me her scraggly bush for a bar
Of chocolate my aunt got from the diplomats store.
I sit while they laugh, their faces lit
Momentarily by the matches' hissing.
They say I'll sing, much better than I did
On all those memory shedding pages.
And I try to convince myself *again*
Is just a word. The same as *encore*, *bis*, *da capo*.

SPANNING

each time   I blink
              memories hunt me
a pack of relentless wild dogs
after my throat
where lungless syllables dream
of roaring
              while they
              their tongues stuck out
              seem but silent
shadows
of the clouds
the wind plays with

              this is not me
              this is not real
              I keep repeating
to other animals
behind the gauze
that graze on indifferently

              my eyes are fixed
on my own shadow already overtaken
its legs up in the air
like those of my wooden horse
after I with one sweep of my hand
decided to win the battle

now if I stop
do not move and do not wink
              will they run by and ahead
and I know

what was to happen
    will have happened
             the glass shards in my cheeks
             the powder odor in my nostrils
             the light blaze in my pupils

enough to make
a hand   flip
the page
        and
        relegate everything to
fugue

MORNING DANCE

He sees her drop
    in front of him
    swaying
    like an exotic dancer
    in the silent air
    still
    not letting go of the bucket
        though water already
        billows over the rim
        a caged beast driven
        by the inertia of motion

    people ahead open
    like petals to the morning sun
    leaving the pavement strewn
    with carts prams makeshift trolleys
    plastic containers pails jugs

He watches the breeze jerk
    a lock of her hair
    exposing the neck and
    a glistening red earthworm
    pulsating blindly toward the ground

He stand over her
    his hands stretched out frozen
    a dance partner of thirty years
    waiting for the curtain to come
    down and the audience crouched
    in the bushes behind jagged walls
    to burst once again into applause

TOMATOES, DOGS AND MIRACLES

I do not know any more
what to put on her to smother
these throbbing welling holes,
my hands all sticky and red
like mother's stuffing
crushed tomatoes into jars
before the first smell of snow.

She touches my hand,
her fingers so cold, so white,
so spectrally clean.

"Please, help me."

I pray to hear the gravel
crackling under car tires,
the door closing—no lights,
no sirens, no screeching
in this pulpous lull outside
that would wake a gunner
haunting the passage
from the stony spire.

"I'm sorry. I'm not
a doctor."

Her milky eyes are
half-closed. For a moment
I think of my dog, his candle
shadow still quivering
on the wall, who used to fool

me with this seeing sleep.

"You're a poet," she whispers.
"Don't you do miracles?"

DEFLOWERING NIGHT

the lightning
unzipping the sky
a glimpse of
the glazed flesh

the wind fingering
an invisible second hand
a scream frozen
in the fallopian tube

how many of them
straddling and whipping
salty searing drops
exploding on her skin

headless clouds fleeing
across the window pane
like sheep to be counted
before the sun flowers again

when all is seen and done
another night should be gone
sleep but sleep my little one
the eyes shall dream of none

UPPER & LOWER

The small wooden box that arrived yesterday
Contains a set of my mother's teeth.

Two pink tortoise shells in the cotton snow.
Unmoving I try to make my eyes stir them

To hear the clucking they made when chewing meat.
As if the illusion could bring my mother back.

I remember seeing in documentaries camp
Survivors' mouths full of stumps and holes.

Now I look the same in the bathroom mirror.
When asked about my scars of war I smile.

So does mother. Probably. Sitting naked on
Some river bank with no plowed-over field

Across where bleached skulls come spring
Rains would plop up and grin at her ghastly.

I wonder whether she wanted to tell me
Something. That that was the way to leave

This place. Toothless. Like a baby.

MOTHERS, FATHERS
AND CHILDREN OF WAR

Constantly denied love passionately
Mother finally became moonstruck.

Standing on the river bank at night
She watched small whirlpools churn war
Leftovers while I hiding in the folds
Of her skirt prayed my heart remain afloat.

Later she taught me to dive
And each time I disappeared in
The greenish film I saw my ivory father
Sitting there playing cards with the moon
Taking swigs from a black brandy bottle.

Many years later she would ask me,
When I sent you down, did you ever see him—
And I never knew whether she was aware
I caught a glimpse of him that very day
Kissing my piano teacher in a rowing boat.

One day she screamed after him,
Why couldn't you have died in the war
Like any other decent human being—
Thin drops of blood trickling from her lip
As if reluctant to stain her white apron.

That night in the cold bedroom I stood
Barefoot at the window writing words
Over words on my glassy breath
That obscured the big stump in the yard

On which father sent chicken heads
Flying off like white birds, I'll wage war
To end all wars and make everyone love you.

LIVING AND DYING

Living is, mother used to say, learning
To understand someone else's suffering.
I asked her once: is dying learning
To suffer one's own understanding?
What a clever boy you are, she said.
Then added: think of living as history,
And dying, what else but poetry.
I smiled having no idea what she meant.

I'm alive but I don't know if I could call it
Living. The game is over. There's no one around.
The theater of operations is quiet. I stare
At the dark screen waiting for my echo
To appear as a fleeting smudged dot. And
This being a poem I can also put in
A pearly moon above the south end of the pit
And a raven flopping around as if trying
To pluck it off the sky and carry it in its beak.

Am I able to understand my own suffering?
Still selfish because I'm afraid of dying?
History I know is no longer made. It's negotiated
By generals in business suits. Or businessmen
Who behave like generals. And if my life
Has been imagined history too is a virtual reality.

Poor mother, so wrong. History never had anything
To do with living. Or, so right. One comes
To learn that by suffering one's own understanding.

That is why the raven has sallied out of the poem
And fixed its spectral eye on my glassy eyeballs.

THE LETTERS CROSSED

You're a survivor, my mother
wrote in her last letter, exiled
by warmongers and betrayed by
her lymphatic vessels, unaware
that I've been translated
into another literal world
with a ratio of one to one
to end up eating dog food
and reading yellow pages
of my useless books
in some roach infested room.

To survive, the dictionary says,
is to continue to live
or exist after the death of:
my own life?—something
I can presume if I take
the *or* to be exclusive.

Would she still consider this
a verbal trick of my fallacious trade?
Strangely enough, in my last letter,
which she has never read,
I said, you are a survivor
if surviving is existing
regardless of and beyond your life.

Was this too stiff fingers' sleight
of hand, similar to her oddly shaped
letters on a painfully rosy paper,
trying vainly to seduce with

fictional twists and turns
a semblance of survival's inclusion?

No answer. Not in the mailbox
that offers me riches if
I have and return the winning number.

SURVIVING TIME

Sitting buried beneath the earth's eye-level
I often wondered what I had been doing
In my mother's womb while she counted
The intervals of cannon drumfire—
Was I marking the breathless respite with her,
Was my heartbeat her beguiling counterpoint—
To mediate the time between two walls

The time to escape as if the mind found a crack
In the hourglass that made the matter diffuse

To be back in a writer's home on the lake
Whose moonless black surface resembled
A huge pot of ink, seated on a wooden chair
Across from two banjos, two frozen eyes removed
From their frame, his daughter lying in fever,
While he, in a surgeon's smock, with a watch
On each wrist, paced between her and my earshot,
Oblivious of everything but our breathing beats

The time to keep in hand, confusing Atropos
With a two-seamed thread and leaving her
In the cellar hanging from the ceiling beam
Like an unskinned hare to yield tender meat

The water breaking through the gasping nebulae
The batteries in my watches gone dead
Dried ink on my fingertips turning red
My figure emerging, the shadow of a gnomon,
I hear my dead mother whisper to me feverishly,
Beware, beware, they fire them at intervals
Of three minutes ten seconds, three ten, three ten

A ONE SENTENCE POEM
(TO BE CARRIED OUT WITH
ONE OR TWO HANDS)

to break down the whys of whos
(not letting history have therapists as final executioners)

to level the wheres of whens
(not waiting for bulldozers to be the final judgement)

I have to survive my own survival

SOMEWHERE ELSE

"A few summers ago the war was somewhere else."

And I was somewhere else. Or so it seemed.
At a safe distance from the confluence of proximities.

After a momentary almost anxious blankness
of the tv screen and before the voice rationalizes
our own absurdity. A bloated corpse floating
down the steaming dawn river. Entangled in branches
like a moth caught in the spider's web.

But I was somewhere else. Salty sea crystals
tickling my skin. My iodized mind eeling
around and between someone's buttocks and breasts.

Then two men in blue overalls. Dragging hurriedly
a limp body. Its feet bouncing off clods
of a fallow to a refrigerator van. Its display ad
showing a wreathed girl with a salami in her arms.
The words beneath Our World Famous Cold Cuts.
Half eaten by rust. Half smeared by mud.

But I was somewhere else. My eyes following
a solitary dolphin that had wandered into
the bay. Swimming so determinedly towards
the land. As if testing its own resolve to live.

That evening I waited alone on the beach.
Sleepless waves burying slowly my numbed feet
in the slimy sand. And I knew the war was
nowhere else but where I stood. Staring at
the flat barren sky in that converging night.

FALLING OUT

Every day we came to the seminary
At noon for bean soup and two slices of bread
Someone was missing from the table
And we knew he'd been killed or had left the city.

Death was discussed in great detail,
Movements retraced, habits guessed at,
Clothing rationalized about, time and weather
Compared, scrutinized and deftly analyzed.

Leaving, conversely, was always generalized,
A bus no one else knew about, a secret tunnel
Everyone heard of, a mad dash across the airport
Runway at the hour a soldier becomes homesick.

And then that painful feeling of being
Forsaken and faithless while the breath
Still struggled to retain the flavor of food
And the mind to erase the notion the figure
Nailed to the wood at the far end of the room
Needed to have its spear wound repainted red.

BAKING BREAD

Beyond everything unreal
Nothing is the only verity

—finding a blind spot
of a mortar shell

lighting the pilot light
as the sniper's eye blinks—

Crazed calculations
Courting involuntary muscles

—as if the body could absorb
the blow and make the brain

disown the pain when the entrails
rise ethereal like batter dough

and a salty crust begins to form
on the burning shivering lips—

The mind striving in vain
To reason with the stomach

—you peer through the oven
window and there's nothing

except a hissing sound and
a fermented breathing essence

that for a moment makes you believe
there must be something beyond nothing—

But what's that got to do
With snipers and mortar shells:

Nothing if you haven't been there

COMING AROUND

every gesture of mine is
a twitch
every smile of mine is
a grimace
every word of mine is
a wound

do you need some counseling
a friend asked
and I sitting upright in the corner
far away from the window
where a bullet could no longer catch
me answered calmly
no I am fine now

and to prove that I walked
straight to the table
a huge platter with
neatly cascading slices of meat
lifted two pieces onto my plate
watching the bloody juice
close the gap silently

the hostess rushing to me
it's so good that after all
that death and hunger
you can eat again normally
don't be shy there's so much more
in the other room and the kitchen

and I step into a ricochet of voices
clutching in my hand a loaf
of bread and smile at everybody
thinking how many days
I could go if I slice it flawlessly

SIMPLE LOGIC

1.

> a beheaded sardine
> between two slices of bread
> in the people's kitchen
>
> I swim in the ocean
> searching for its head
> a rooster's floats by
> I eat it but am still late
> for the new world order

2.

Question:
> Where do refugees go?

Answer:
> Certainly not to heaven.

Reasons for Denial:
> No one to sponsor them there.

3.

> I crouch in the bushes
> twisting a bird's neck
> suppressing its instinct to dart
> out and betray my presence
>
> the light trims the tongues
> of leaves but I'm so close
> to the earth I can smell my breath
> already rotting into eternity

4.
I am tired of writing
About my survival
Dissecting dumb luck
To find some logic.

On this island I am
Supposed to be at peace
With symmetrical hedges
Indubious arrows on the pavement
And people I tell that after
Having been buried I must
Come from heaven.

Have I fulfilled the terms
Of my contract? Am I finally
Ready? Free at last,

God?

THE LANGUAGE OF DREAMS

Do you dream in this language,
Someone once asked me.
I do not dream at all; I watch
A film every night with my eyes
Shut, the same shadow images
That pulsate on walls in another room.

The train clatters by shaking my bed;
I clutch the ticket in my hand,
Sure to be the first to give it
To the conductor in this empty carriage.

And I know that will not be enough,
For someone behind him will speak out,
Dokumenten. Papers. Ausweis.

My face that runs moon-like behind
The window pane through burned-out
Houses and scrawny tree crowns
Holds its forefinger on my lips.

And I see my specter go by on a train,
Crouching under the table, a child
Once again playing hide-and-seek
With the shells that will tag my sweat,
My counted sheep already blown to bits.

One dreams in a language
That feels his pain, no more no less.

FORGETTING AND FORGIVING

(A Statement)
Of forgetting
an impassive horizontal motion
of a limpid glove, to the left or
to the right, a relentless circular
movement of a morsel of bread
trying in vain to herd brownish sludge
on a wobbly aluminum plate
and forgiving
those who put their memory to sleep
ready to claim they never squashed a fly
never whipped their white stallion
never neglected their flower garden
The balance is
a dead weight between madness and sanity.

(An Explanation)
Sanity is to forget a whoosh of air faster
Than my brain imaging the room
Where nothing stirred and then was erased
By easter light that burned black in my pupils,
To forget the cheapness of being alive
While a dog was dying silently, the only screams
Locked in his eyes, after I'd clapped my hands
Daring him to cross the street with a sign Beware
Of Sniper scribbled on a cardbox that also warned
In another life Fragile Do Not Tumble.

Madness is to have to forgive those who don't
Remember what I am supposed to forget,
Not to walk on one side of the street only

Not to flinch whenever standing at the window
Not to lie in bed awake because all is too quiet.

(A Gloss)
If history forgets for the sake of brevity.
If time forgives for the sake of healing.

BLIND WALK

The glass doors open with a jerk.
I start to walk. I try not to think.
My head is tilted, as if avoiding
a blow. The surge of blood
pushing my thoughts against the right
wall of the skull. There's a drum
in my temple, armless pounding.
Time is jammed in this raw
membrane of voiceless rhythms.
An unfinished sentence. A child
dragged by his mother keeps glancing
at me, then sticks his blue tongue
out. My mind goes through the same
motion my lips turn into a smile.
I want his mother to look at me.
Are we both from the same city?
Did we stand in the same mute line
for a blanket or a bucket of water?
Are we both alive in this sterile
corridor flanked by Remy Martin
and Rado ads because we didn't know
better? Already overtaken by
a group of young men, laughing and
jostling, with duty free bags in
their hands, muzzled cameras slung
over their shoulders. A horse-faced
old man with a unicef bag, a toy gun
barrel protruding out, catches up
with her and like an animal sensing

the approach she turns, her eyes
white like two hard boiled eggs.
He motions to me to move past them.
I hear him whisper, Do you know
who's here…? I strain my ears.
It's him, I tell you…. The poet.
I quicken my pace and turning
the corner I look at the kid again.
The same blue tongue now blows
a huge pink bubble that goes bang.
His mother's head jerks slightly.
Will he reappear ten years from
now to put me down? Knowing
that I will be in some corridor
moving like a bat caught in
the blinding unechoing light.

A TALE

Thousand and one nights away
In a city where all windows had glaucoma
And hunger was a cannibal dancing in the brain,
I stole voraciously candles and matches
To copy the death-bed edition
Of *Leaves of Grass* in minuscule letters
Of another language and make it lighter
In a battered vinyl case when lugged
Across the powder bleached field.

My Barthelmes and Malamuds left behind,
And my Styrons, Bellows, Doctorows, now
Next to someone's tomatoes and kidney beans.

Bits and pieces of my life are
Being sold on the side of a muddy road.

/Post-
Word/

He appears out of a distant past. Old acquaintances, we shake hands, work together. History and consciousness intermingle, seep into each other like fall and redemption.

His present is uncertain, but the issue is his immediate past. Rumors, pictures, words bear vague testimony to something brutal, monstrous, a war never to be forgiven. Packages in the mail containing dentures, bodices, other memento mori sent by war-crazed relatives do not let him forget. The only consolation: the house of language and logic, no matter how short the lease, full of draughts, empty of sleep...

1
Do we need Mario to bring Bosnia into our living rooms? Or shall we obscenely claim we have our own Bosnias, the Bosnias of our hearts, the Bosnias of our minds? You, you stay out of here. Or if you must be with us, Shut up!

2
Must we merely pretend? That as we struggle to cease being mere readers of the news or voyeurs of catastrophe and move

to being witnesses, we're in the cellars of Sarajevo watched by a thousand bullet eyes? And look at the long arms of the mortar shells. How they extend themselves to reach out and touch someone! Did I say "someone"? Could it be me? Is there a way not to pretend?

3

The year begins in the mind. As the old one ends, also in the mind.

Perhaps we're still years away from Jozef Klem's arche-illogical discovery (in the mind) of MSMS.

Who is it who comes to me, an ms. in his hand? Is it the future Jozef Klem conditionally emerging in the mind's simple present from an indefinite past? He's made of flesh and bone. I know he is (as they say in these parts) "for real." I have put my metaphoric hand in his side. He calls himself MS. He's both father and son of Jozef Klem. He's (only) as real as all things in time— a specter, a metaphor. "Look here," he says, raising his hand, "This here is *Manus* and this *Scriptus*" and holding his hand and his manuscript up alternately, moving them up and down like a robotic juggler or like the warning signal at a railway crossing gone haywire, he shouts, "This *manus* clawed out this *scriptus* first on the dank walls of the mind's caves, then in the cellar of a bombed apartment in Sarajevo, then under the light screaming in through a skylight in Hempstead, then... and then... and then..." He deposits it in my hand, a charred baby. It is an ms. called MSMS by one MS. I suffocate in the prison house of broken letters and shattered syllables.

I turn away for relief, for space and time. I reach for the Manu Smriti, an ms. from the dawn of my own ancient India. I read about the great cycles of time: Krita 1,728,000 years long; Treta 1,296,000; Dvapara 864,000 and Kali 432,000 human years. How dwarfish the year 1995 looks or for that matter the year 2028. Here I read about origin and apocalypse, about the nature of things, about eternal law: War is good in its own right, it says. Though grim, it is an exciting sport. Sometimes you must engage in it as a religious duty. So says the Manu Smriti.

"See," screams MS, "I told you so! It's all in here, in my ms., in my MSMS!"

A new age begins in the mind... the war rages on in the mind...

4
A Select Chronology:

Pre-1995
shells burst 10 meters away / he escapes / wall falls on him / he's pulled out / manages to leave / police take dog away

Bosnia's a bonfire of profanities / his books are burnt / a minor matter

Nassau / news of mother / she will smile again / will it be out of a photo-graph or a snap-shot?

gets job / loses job / gets it back / to have and to hold / till

judge and jury concur: he's a lifer

August 95
A famous writer calls to say he finds the book moving but isn't qualified to say it! He's only a novelist...

November 95
Blues for MSMS are back / need to make changes / printer breaks.

December 95
Mario needs to batten down the hatch / too much freedom, too much of a draught / lifts air conditioner out and breaks his back / life's going to get him one way or another / who knows about death?

Production manager at Patterson Printing rams car into tree / further delays

The book arrives

I open book / margins are off / I open book / pages are missing / I open my eyes / everything is off / I open my eyes / the world is missing

This is not news for Mario

January 96
Blizzard / Mario's car is buried

Blizzard / Mario's buried

A friend buys a copy of the book and is confused by the cover description: is the poet alive or dead? I tell her it's not clear but it could be a cover up. The poet from under the snow, brooding among the shoots of lilac: "Life's a cover up."

Newspaper headline slashed at the last minute by front page compositor:

They found the man / but weren't sure / if he was alive or dead...

March 96
Marvin, an old friend: Your book instructs me. (But don't quote me... You know, a poet's word means nothing.)

Jeremy: Your words can't leave anyone passive.

Chris: I'm enjoying it a great deal—moving, real, very imaginative in its format.

Max (from England): To see these poems on the page confirms the memory I have of someone who, literally, sees through everything.

Letters, postcards—spring generosities.

April 96
Blizzard / Book is buried

5
Helen Vendler says that Seamus Heaney in his *The Redress of Poetry* carries on an internal quarrel—between the urgency of witness and the urgency of delight.

A question for Mario: Is there delight in retrieving a severed arm?

6
Lyrical Act I:

"The first person, free-verse, lyric narrative poem of my earlier years has given way to a work which has desired its own bodying forth: polyphonic, broken, haunted, and in ruins, with no possibility of restoration." Carolyn Forché describing her *Angel of History*.

Lyrical Act II:

In the dark times, will there also be singing?
Yes, there will be singing.
About the dark times.

Bertolt Brecht

Finale:

"Shell them till they're on the edge of madness." Ratko Mladic, the Bosnian Serb general, ordering his men on the hills surrounding Sarajevo.

7

"The vast open-pit iron mine, the hulks of ore-processing machinery and the bulldozers lie blanketed in snow, but the scene is not abandoned... The mining complex... central collection point and hiding place for thousands of corpses... The Bosnian Serbs, according to non-Serb miners in the town, are exhuming the remains of victims from numerous mass graves in the area and transferring the bodies to this mine, where they are often mangled in old mining equipment, doused with chemicals and reburied under tons of debris in the open pits." Chris Hedges, NY Times

Question: What does this have to do with Mario's poetry? With poetry? Is this what poetry is: a settling of old scores? a resettlement? tamping the earth over hasty graves for a new house?

8

How dare I say it? But I must: we're all survivors here. Should we not realize at a deep level that Mario, a survivor of the war in Bosnia, has only a version of our own stories to tell?

A survivor is one who's escaped with his imagination in tact— bruised and battered may be, but still alive. These poems, forged in the heart of the Olympic hell, are the signs of Mario's survival. And, by extension, maybe by a great stretch of the imagination, they are the dark songs of our own survival.

9

Bosnia: One Big Yawn. Harper's, February 1996.

An e-mail sent last July to the *Miami Herald* by Doug Clifton, the paper's executive director: "If anyone has an idea on what to do with the Bosnia story, I welcome it. I am embarrassed to say I long ago stopped reading this story of enormous human tragedy and significant global consequence. Why is that? Some of it is my global failure. I'm callous, parochial, and maybe even stupid. But more of it may be my—our—professional failure... Yes, I care about man's inhumanity to man, but I care more about whether this latest event brings the world or the U.S. closer to the brink. A reader—even a high-minded, liberal-thinking one with a worldview— wants to know, 'What does this mean to me?'"

10

News of mass graves in Serb-held Bosnia. Ljubija: mines crammed with dead bodies. NATO doesn't think it's its duty to investigate.

A writers' group in Ridgefield looks at *Mothers, Shoes*... No sales, no interest. Is Bosnia too much with us?

We have our own wars, our own mines, our own dead bodies, words, words, words. They'll stink when you exhume them. These words. They are unrecognizable. But they all point to the same horror. We have our internal wars. Especially us women. You should know.

Will you come down with me into these mines? We are not peace keepers. We are not grave diggers. We are in the business of exhuming bawdy words like war, genocide, racism, hate, fear...

11

Give us a break. We are overloaded. Too much on our plate. Can't feel. In denial. Ecological disaster. Entropy. The whole thing's winding down. Why worry about short-term slaughter? Galaxies multiply by the million. And watch out! The sperm count's down, way down. What are a few miserable Muslims in Bosnia when the whole species is on the brink?

12

How do we respond to pain, speak of pain when at worst our

pain is psychological? Have we been bombed out of our cellars? thrown out of our villages? Have we fled from plagues?

But what nonsense! We have our own wars.

13
Elaine Scarry says those who are in pain have no language. We must speak, then, you and I, while we can.

14
I don't mean to steal Mario's thunder, his shell fire, his pain, his loss of his books, dog, mother, world. But I must say, however mutely, that we too are survivors. And as survivors we have a choice, such as it is, to live or to surrender. It makes sense for us to gather here to listen to Mario, for once he escaped the shells and falling walls, he cast his lot in favor of the living. You see this, among other things, in his words, in his imagination that staggers forward.

Jozef Klem, the mysterious figure, archaeologist, "discovers" this manuscript in the year 2028. Does this book then contain the shape of our present as the future will discover it. Is this how we will be remembered? Is this how we will remember?

15
Christopher Merrill, who recently returned from Sarajevo says: "We must write as witnesses, not watchers. The difference between witnessing and watching is a function of the imagination. First we watch, and then, if our imaginations are sufficiently engaged, we witness..." In this light, consider *Mothers, Shoes...*

16
"Why do we write? Does it make any sense to document the war at all, when it is bound to happen again? My own experience with this war tells me that to write is, above all, to try to establish some kind of order in chaos. In a general sense, writing itself is the proof that human beings can behave rationally, and this might be the only purpose. As it is possible to kill, it is possible to write....

"But I think we should give up the illusion that we learn from any of these experiences. We don't. On the other hand, if war is the negation of humanity, documentary prose is its affirmation. More than that, I am afraid we should not hope for, either as writers or as human beings..."

Slavenka Drakulic
Afterword to *Sarajevo, Exodus of a City* by Dzevad Karahasan

17

Who am I to deny your claim that you have the killing fields within you? Here look at our Bosnias, our inner cities, you say. Here, peer into my heart of darkness, if you care to.

But we're not here to compete: who has the greatest sorrow? who has the deepest pain? We're here to make sense, perhaps, see the light. Slavenka Drakulic trying to make some sense of the dismemberment of Sarajevo reads Primo Levi's memoir, *Survival in Auschwitz*. We must remember the horrors of war and genocide in order not to repeat them, Levi urges. Fifty years later, the very same generation that heard the stories of Auschwitz sees the destruction of Sarajevo. So what use are warnings? Indeed, what use words? what use is poetry?

To shape momentary order out of chaos, to hope past the death of reason... This must suffice, for there are no guarantees we will not kill again, absolutely no guarantees that we will not forget again...

In the meanwhile, we live in the meanwhile

and seek the promise of love, the protection of love...

In a letter to his Serbian wife separated from him by war, Dzevad Karahasan, a Muslim, writes: "My dear, beautiful, only one: ...In the same way that it has built bridges in time, connecting my time with yours, our love has built a wall around us in space..."

So we too try to build bridges with our very local love (perhaps the only one that matters,) hoping that bridges do not meet the same fate as the one recently destroyed in Mostar...

and while building them sing in these dark times...

in the meanwhile...

18

Mario, Maria and I walk in the New Canaan Nature Center. It's a beautiful day—sunny, crisp and dry. We walk on well-padded paths, admire an occasional dead sculpture of a tree amid the burgeoning new foliage, stand beside ponds deep red with undredged weed. "It's so quiet here," Maria says, this woman who has picked her way through the rubble of Sarajevo, "so quiet and beautiful. You could kill someone and no one would know it."

We walk through a vine arbor, across a meadow rippling with Queen Anne Lace and little pink blossoms, and stop briefly at a ramshackle shed stocked with a press, extruder, sieve and other implements for making maple syrup. Maria is suddenly frozen at the sight of something she sees on the black wall. She gasps. "Ah, awful, I don't want to see them ever again," she exclaims, a mixture of pain and horror in her face, as she points to a bulging cluster of empty plastic milk cartons that hang on the wooden wall. Mario's silence screams.

Sarajevo comes to mind, a broken sofa in an open field, women in rags trudging along battered walls with empty milk canisters foraging for water.

The village of Trapaeng Sva in Cambodia flashes across the eye with its by now famous mounds of skulls. With some effort I could retrieve these images—from my own private hoard of clippings! And shed some light as they burn one by one...

19

The Unitarians have invited Mario to do a service. A poetry reading as religious ritual. The death of priests is the birth of poets. (Swallow hard!) The colorful pennants draping the pillars proclaim the democracy of gods and faiths.

I sit on the red velvet throne next to Mario. I whisper to him: The book is real. Proof: it can be burnt.

20

Mario prefaces a poem: I like to walk. I was terrified of losing my legs. Losing my life would have been less painful.

How I love hierarchies!

21

With some luck one may dodge bullets, survive bursting shells.
But how to survive the thunderous silence of the American lite-
rati... A problem for the gods...

22

He held their hand, in a manner of speaking, as they came one
by one to Sarajevo on their poetry tours, held them by the hand
and took them through the streets of this great city. Bell and
Levis, Ashbery and the golden Orr. The great Bellows, Dickeys
and Doctorows followed not far behind in the back lanes of his
mind. In a manner of speaking...

Did they walk together in the elegant evenings as the cafe lights
came on one by one talking of war and the death of civilization,
the uses and futility of literature, of the bankruptcy of the old
world and the wasteland that is the new? In and out of muse-
ums, libraries, cafes and, perhaps to relieve the tedium of cul-
ture and soulful things, quick little dives into bordellos with
screens, the colors of humanity.

Now that he's a guest in their ample land, the hosts are absent.
There's a sign on the door: Out to Lunch. One of them calls:
"Some day you and I must go back to Sarajevo and visit the old
haunts. Perhaps return to that wall at Vraca. Those Jewish fami-
lies. Where did they disappear? Those thousand names. They
haunt me."

23

Ask not for whom...
It tolls for thee Bell
And Schulman fulla
Grace and sh—

24

The desk in front of me is a note pad for desultory spirits. Screech-
ing weasel likes me, says one. Let me stay with that. Why is the
weasel screeching? Do you know how hopeless I feel right now?
I'm choking. I don't have anything to say. Mario was tremen-
dous. I was riveted to his eyes that went up to the ceiling be-
tween words—as if there was a spirit crouching up there among

the girders and beams, a mean-spirited little gargoyle that controlled the destinies of men. So he'd look up between words praying silently. Now don't piss on my words, don't spit, shit, stomp on my words. They're all I have. But I didn't see anything up there.

25
Mario's back from Northampton—the great consortium of thought, the Five College Area. He read at Broadside, in the heart of the town. Missing the bookstore is like wandering in the Vatican and missing St. Peter's. It was a balmy spring day. Mario read to an audience of seven: one of them seemed to be a stray who meant to be in Civitanova but found himself on the bloody side of the Adriatic!

26
"War's wonderful! If you survive it! Then you can talk about it." (Eerie laughter.) "Even have fun with it." I think: Life's wonderful. If you survive it!

Mario talks about getting to the point when he must live on a slice of bread a day. Ah, yes, you can spend a whole day eating that one slice. Morsel by morsel, grain by grain. After a while, you know you're not eating the bread but the very thought of it.

A student comes to Mario after his reading: "You did good!" she says with a beaming face. Yes, Mario did good! And today he wants to die. I'm merely recording. Why? Because I have nothing better to do? When will I stop this pecking at words amid this widescattering of meaning? It would be better, wouldn't it, to stand out in the spring sun, open oneself up in a large gesture of being extended on the cross, seemingly embracing the world while being nailed on it, and let oneself be scattered, not be gathered, but scattered like shimmering nebulae?

27
I've lost Mario in the shuffle of life
Mario's lost Mario in the shuffle of life
Mario, me, shuffle, life, lost,
repeat (andante) ad infinitum

28

How tragic that he's just one of the cards in the deck. There the King and the lowly 2 are both shovelled over by the Ace of Spades. In all of this it seems the only redemption is to be the Joker pfft psss outa da door slip and slide and sleight of hand foot in the mouth bbbggg arrrgh puff of smoke into thy hands I com... why hast thou forsak... *consummatum datum est...*

29

A reading at a major university in Connecticut:

Outside on the green, the rock band rocks the hot dogs sizzle young boys and girls burst in their bodies made by birth for death. Inside the poet dies words are bad breath questions are asked so that silence may not embarrass coffee and pastry are superior the only real things. Mario is unloosed. No podium. His arms and hands extend his words, his crossed feet, the swaggered bend of hip and point of beard give the words new life within death. One in the audience, a personage, huddles in the chair. She pulls her legs up to her chin. She sits at 45 degrees to the poet, her gaze trapped like a fugitive in the right corner of room. She pulls up her knees, higher, foetal. I turn to my friend and ask her in a scribbled note if this attendee, this dignitary, is an informal person. She says no. I say Then she's depressed. Mario's poems evaporate before the misery of this woman who has gone back into the womb to be buried. There are wars and wars. We must choose. The choice is no more difficult than the excruciation of facing gouda and brie and blue and cheddar and havarti all in a space of a few capitalist inches.

30

With a church group in Stamford:

We're back. A huge billboard in the heart of downtown proclaims a reading by Bosnian Poet, Mario Susko etc. The coffee houses were filled in Camus' Oran at the height of the plague. So too here, they are filled, and the lights, the warmth and the aromas seduce. A plague on poets. Poets are the plague. Dead rats. Get under your skin. Damn them. But not so inside. Tall willowy women with glowing intentions receive us. We are back, Bosnian Hardy and Indian Laurel, Unlucky and Unpozzo. They are reverential. Church goers are like that. They have moved beyond the politics of God. God's everywhere and everything. Instead of the Credo we listen to the Waves of the Danube. The space is empty. What might Pascal have said! The women with hearts as wide as ocean liners tell us they sent out 3000 announcements: to the New Home Owners' Association, to the Antique Dealers' Guild, and to the Gold Tooth Club. The women are disappointed. A poet deserves better. We say Nonsense! We are honored! There's no better audience than the emptiness of a godless crypt; there's no better hearing but within silence. The poet breaks the silence with his words. To break bread is a higher calling, of course.

31
Mario hears that some people across the big water are nervous about *Mothers, Shoes...* because they think that it's some YUgoslavian publishing firm, a crypto-nationalist Serbian enterprise: YUganta. Here's the last straw. Why is the camel still standing up? Maybe it never learned the expression, "the straw that broke the camel's back." If you don't hear about death, you may live for ever. Ergo, to live, then, is not to know "death."

32
I have three hours to kill in Harvard Square. I step into Grolier Poetry Book Shop. Louisa Solano scowls in front of her cluttered register. She makes and breaks poets. Grolier: the St. Peter's (or at least the Sistine Chapel) of poetry in the US. 14,000 titles. Solano growls: the poets are the worst customers. They don't buy; they kibbitz. I say that after all hers is a labor of love. She mutters, "It was," and looks up at me with wistful eyes signalling the death of culture. I tell her that I'm there to track down our latest book, *Mothers, Shoes...* She says it's on the center table with Szymborska and the rest. I forage but don't see it. Lost again, in the mass of words and titles and stunning covers, piles of souls, mounds of poets eating their hearts out. I search relentlessly. The poet of my book may be lost, but his book must be found. My mission in life: finding lost souls, including my own. After an hour (Solano grumbling the whole time) I spot Mario's book behind the counter, out of reach of the world. I exclaim and lodge a mild complaint. She grunts saying it was a

new hand who shelved the latest books. I say it belongs in war poetry, and step out into the cold to look for lunch. An hour later I'm back. Mario's book is between Heaney's *Selected Poems* (celebrating and mourning Irish blood) and Forche's anthology *Against Forgetting* which is a poetic mausoleum to the horrors of history, an act of fierce memorializing. Between the two, Mario bristles, a befanged thing amid armored vision... No, between the two Mario nestles, a child and parent of the poetic gesture which is, after all is said done, the act of making nothing of death...

33
Anticipating a question from the editors at Poets & Writers—there's always a question about war and love—Peggy Heinrich, the writer of a piece on Mario, feels compelled to assure them there's love here in this war poetry: "...Sunny, the dog, for one; the people in the marketplace—all the pain he suffers from observing people in misery is because of and reflects love."

34
Love's not enough.

P&W editors to Heinrich: The poet needs to be fleshed out.

Heinrich to me: They say the poet needs to be fleshed out.

I to myself: Yes, the poet needs to be fleshed out here in a culture that does not understand O that this too too solid flesh would melt... Why, flesh is the only thing that signifies, that testifies, that reifies, that validates, that inaugurates, that coagulates, that incarnates reality. And what may I ask happens to the spirit? What spirit? In a place where the body has no soul, even the soul is seen as body.

An afterthought: Did I perhaps mishear what Heinrich said to me? Did she perhaps say that P&W said to her that the poet needs to be flushed out? In either case, we face an impossibility. This poet, being dead, cannot, by definition, be fleshed out and, again, being dead, cannot be flushed out since in his present state he doesn't even qualify as "solid waste."

35

Mario must produce "three sentences" which declare the precariousness of his status... so his lawyer can sign the document... so the college can give him back what was his by years of service—tenure.

"Three sentences" carry more weight than *Mothers, Shoes*... They can make waves. The poetry is mere driftwood amid the flotsam. Or... is it perhaps a message in a bottle to be picked up by a Jozef Klem who combs the beaches for news of past and long-dead worlds?

36

Do not call me Jozef Klem. Ishmael is another matter. I am a counsel wolf demoted to being a fox for having lost the audience I never had. I give counsel now at reduced rates. The wind listens and scatters it across the seven seas. The fish are my saviors: eternally they carry in their little and big bellies the breath of my words along with deathless plutonium.

37

He lost his shirt in Bosnia, and with it his soul. Tell me (you who know everything) if there's anything else he might have lost; I'll add it to the inventory of missing things. He struggles now to find his soul in a culture where there's none to be found. ("But that's so unfair," I hear them scream, perhaps with some justice, "he's alive! Isn't that enough?!")

38

(The poet) is oppressed by a burden which he must bring to birth in order to obtain relief. Or, to change the figure of speech, he is haunted by a demon, a demon against which he feels powerless, because in its first manifestation it has no face, no name, nothing; and the words, the poem he makes are a kind of exorcism of this demon. In other words again, he is going to all that trouble, not to communicate with anyone, but to gain relief from acute discomfort; and when the words are finally arranged in the right way—or in what he comes to accept as the best possible arrangement he can find—he may experience a moment of appeasement, of absolution and of something very near to annihilation, which is itself indescribable.

T.S. Eliot

39

Hiss-tory (sic): history in the wake of a just-launched mortar shell before it hits ground zero.

Conversation heard in a snake pit:

Who did it?

Not me.

Who then?

The snake did it.

What the hell d'ya mean?

Wha...?

We're all snakes in here, you fatass dumbo!

40

M calls to say he just finished perhaps his strongest poem ever. Among other things, it alludes to the universe and to James Dickey and daughter. Two days later, he opens the newspaper and reads of Dickey passing away.

Is death the order of the universe and the life of poetry merely the way to get there?

41

Counsel from a well-meaning friend:

Forego honoraria; engage in a good-will building strategy; not realistic nor very possible to get honoraria at this time of nonentity; I agree even minor poets should be given honoraria, but imagine such a thing happening on this side of parousia!

42

A prescription for goodwill building:

Hug your anonymity as you'd hug your nakedness.

Stand before an audience and strip. Show them all you've got.

Spill your guts into a mixing bowl. Use swilling motion of snout to stir with appropriate grunts. Let the blood clots rise. A delicacy.

Inner organs need special preparation. Marinate in tangy commentary.

Let them have the liver and the spleen. Tell them the heart's not for sale until the hard cover's out of print.

And as for that most private of all delicacies: rub it with olive oil and wrap it in a fig leaf. Thus preserved, the stock of this seminal item will steadily rise beyond the curve of all publishing dreams.

End on a Latin note: Say goodbye to honoraria and read gratis.

43

The poet wears black. I, his shadow, wear black too. His laugh is absurd brass, mine spasmodic tin. Together we're ready to face a crowd, he in the spotlight and I on the sidelines. It's an act we've polished smooth like a black pebble. They can roll us in their mouth like round hard candy. But not before they've heard his bloody words and survived my silence.

44

I prepare to introduce the poet. End of story: I do not introduce the poet. This is an account of what was thought in between: They say, these new immigrants, their bodies are here but their souls are back home. What then is this land of immigrants: mere bodies with displaced souls? Here enters the poet, the worker of miracles. He says, "Listen to me. I am the healer of divisions. I create something out of nothing. I create a home where the heart is not. My art is the art of reclaiming the heart. It is a bitter miracle I work. Poetry is the act of acknowledging the heart's not here."

45

"Did she say I am a war poet? But every poet is. There's always a war somewhere. There's always a poet to sing of it. Without him who would know what war is or for that matter what reality is?"

46

"Maybe they'll come in droves," I say, "and suck up the books like honey from a loaded hive." I wish.

He warns, "Don't push the illusion too far. It may become real."

47

"In a few minutes I'll be done with reading my poems. Then you can leave and forget me." In a few days, in a few years... But until then, shall we fill space and time with the sound of our voices and the soul of our being so that on that day of doom when the four horses snort and the trumpets blare it shall be said, "They were mere voyagers on this earth, yet they left in their wake of bloodclot... what?... stardust."

On the way back from the reading, we drive by St. John's Cemetery. "I love cemeteries, especially after a reading. They remind me of what's what." I catch the corners of this statement and raise it, a tent for the Last Judgment. All shall be gathered under the four trumpeting syllables of poetry.

48

From "entrails/rise over like kneaded yeast dough" to "entrails/rise weightless like battered dough" to finally "entrails/rise ethereal like battered dough"—Mario nails it. Finally. "Baking Bread" is done. Done for?! He's poised at the edge of a chasm of experience. He must find honest ways of naming it, courageous ways of incarnating it. He must be realistic in the process yet write poetry, which for him is the language of compression (as in "collapsed lungs" which is what happens when you crash into reality at a zillion miles per hour. Writing below zero.) He must find the language to do justice to his historical moment, that will dare to speak from within the soul of darkness.

I too stand at the edge of experience. It too is a chasm. Not of mortar-blighted façades, shelled marketplaces, bombed-out stadia, but of inner collapse, an inner sanctum emptied of any meaning, of anything that matters. My experience is language. I do not go in search of words to express what I know and do not know. I fall into language. And pray. That it will not suck me whole into its nefarious designs but let me float upward on its balmy currents into light or at least to the possibility of light. And once, with some grace and luck, that's achieved, what shall I do? Blink? One blink per every little angel that flies across my vision, one blink per every sick dog that can barely drag itself out of its own pisspool.

At Mario's Maria throws up her hands. She says it's too much. He talks about guns. She says, "Naaa, just something to drink will do." This discussion of suicide laces the wonderful spinach soup she's made and homemade bread. You bake it for sixty years and you'll know how to do it. It's all a matter of touch. Instinct bred by time. I think of poetry, its life and death strands, how they are woven inextricably together. Unravel the one and the other is without its support and spine. Twin parasites these, not on a host unless the host is the Nothing of the poet's imagination. I say there's still something left to life, and poetry, its search for meaning... I swallow hard as I say it, stuff my mouth with thickly buttered bread. Bread's better than words that merely create a vague and precarious bridge to nowhere. The bread has a definite path to follow through the narrow passage into the labyrinthine gut to final release as the nightsoil, the very stuff of stars...

49
"Eerie with shattered beauty, the burned ruins of Bosnia's national library have stood for the last four years as a wrenching symbol of an attempt to destroy a city and its culture.

"Now the gouged granite columns, the crumbling crenelated trim and the once resplendent copper cupola, shredded like lacework, stand for something else: the sluggishness of the reconstruction of Sarajevo...

"In May 1992, the Serbs shelled the Sarajevo Oriental Institute, devastating a collection of medieval literature in Arabic, Persian and Turkish and priceless works in four alphabets—Latin, Arabic, Cyrillic and an alphabet that predated Cyrillic, known as Old Bosnian..." *NYT*, 8/12/96

Mario and I continue to write. Our minds are libraries in ruins. The likes of Enes Kujundzic stand pensively before these ruins and think of desperate reconstructive projects. Ms. Lorkovic might say, "We should preserve the ruined choirs and sanctums just as they are, and build the new library, a bright and airy monument. Let the old be a memorial..."

50

The poet's asked to serve on the jury. Is he qualified? Does it matter? And isn't he alive? They don't know the jury's out on him. He tells them he's not alive. Serve, they say. That's an order. Join the bench of the living dead.

I am asked to judge. I forget momentarily that death judges me. This amnesia is perhaps what we call life. And poetry.

But this is sheer nonsense in this country, the Mecca of Matter. There is no amnesia here for that implies there was once memory, remembrances, a past.

51

"My mind has grown a mind of its own," he starts his poem. Possibilities open up where others are ending. This may be a more humane alternative to cloning; the freedom of the second or über or super mind holds out more than the xerox syndrome, mere duplication. Poetry is the act of the mind overcoming itself. It is, after all's said and done, the way to hope and the way to be human, that is, split between hope and despair, split unredeemably, which is our last consolation—that we will never succumb to the one ultimate datum of sameness. Poetry, the dark flower of freedom that splits, like Williams' saxifrage, the rock of thisness. "I want that!" a child cries. The poet is a child, forever crying for... thatness.

52

The poet doesn't sleep. Now it is the war with words. Maria says, "You need a tragedy to live." The good woman then serves cold kidney bean soup, cheese and meat garnished with a sprig of tragedy. The poet eats it hungrily and feels he can live another day. I eat and watch and wait. I am the one doomed to make note of everything—this poet's alimentary passages, that one's insomnia, this one's deadly wrestle with words, even the inscrutable machinations of the one they call God.

53

Via X via Y via Z the following falls into my hands:

The old man was selling books on Marshall Tito Boulevard—Richard Howard's *Alone with America*, Randall Jarrell's *Poetry and the Age*, John Ashbery's *A Wave*: a curious assortment for a bookseller who spoke no English. Zvonko opened Ashbery's collection of poems, read the inscription and nodded. Here were the remains of Mario Susko's library, he said... "A dirty business," Zvonko muttered. "Do you need a copy of *A Wave*? Look: only three marks. What a deal."

from Christopher Merrill's "In the Unreal City", *Double Take* 2:4, Fall 1996.

That the poet ends his poem, "A Tale", with the words: "Bits and pieces of my life are / Being sold on the side of a muddy road" must not impel the reader into a simply tragic interpretation of the event on the famous boulevard in Sarajevo. First, there's the diurnal motion of the earth to consider: personal tragedy turns inevitably into cosmic farce, if not comedy. Second, there are the statements the poet has sprinkled about his circular path: in sum, that the act of writing is the act of living and loving without fully knowing why. He writes. The old man sells bras, bottles, and books. Neither sells out. That ultimately is why the sun rises at the appointed hour and the moon quickens us with desire.

54

Jozef, Mario, and Ralph now start, what shall we call it, their dance of life or death or death in life. The last two, though alive, are dead; the first never existed though is fully alive. This is the phantasmagoric world of poetry. Then again, this is the world, period, phantasmic to its core. You who live in these United States where one lives out a fantasy, ought to know this better than anyone else. Your bodies and minds, your malls and markets, your amusement parks and industrial estates, your e-z passes and super highways, your weight reduction plans and high caloric intakes, your silicon breasts and artificial hearts are all within the realm of real fantasy. So you are all poets like us two who are dead though alive. You should have no difficulty following this poet whose mind is growing a mind of its own even as this country is in the act of cloning itself so one half can shadow the other, call names, kill, erase while the other rises phoenix-fashion, like the poet from out of the ashes of his poems. Do not douse us with water; rather, fan us alive, we beg of you.

Ralph Nazareth

ABOUT THE AUTHOR

Mario Susko, a witness and survivor of the war in Bosnia, left the city of Sarajevo in March of 1993 and came to the US in November of that year. He received his M.A. and Ph.D. from SUNY at Stony Brook in the 1970's and has taught over the years at the Univeristy of Sarajevo and Nassau Community College on Long Island. He has published 58 books, 16 of which are his volumes of poems. Other books of his include editions and translations of leading American writers—Saul Bellow, E. L. Doctorow, William Styron, Kurt Vonnegut, Bernard Malamud, Donald Barthelme, James Baldwin, Theodore Roethke, e. e. cummings among others.